Federico García Lorca: Blood Wedding
(Bodas de Sangre)
In a version by Ted Hughes

Federico García Lorca was born in Fuente Vaqueros, near Granada, in 1898, the eldest son of a prosperous farmer.

Lorca's family moved to Granada in 1909. After unenthusiastically studying law for four years at the University of Granada, Lorca was led by his passion for music and literature to Madrid's celebrated Residence for Students, a prestigious educational institution modelled on the Oxbridge colleges of Britain. Here he remained for ten years, developing close friendships with leading members of a vibrant avant-garde movement, including, among others, the young Salvador Dali.

In 1929, Lorca left Madrid for New York and after an unhappy year he briefly moved to Cuba, before returning to Spain in 1930. His return coincided with the election of a republican government and a new atmosphere of artistic freedom. This gave Lorca's talents the freedom to develop as never before and led to his appointment as director of La Barraca, an innovative government-sponsored touring theatre company. During a hectic and adventurous five years with La Barraca, Lorca established himself as the most popular Spanish playwright of his day. He was able to perform classic Spanish plays to both rural and city audiences whilst developing his own work and unique style, integrating performance, music and dance. It was during this exciting time, Lorca, inspired by newspaper reports about a mysterious murder, wrote and staged *Blood Wedding*.

This time of artistic freedom was not destined to last, and in 1936 Franco's military insurrection led to the outbreak of the Civil War. When rebel troops occupied Granada, Lorca, suspected of republican sympathies and despised by some for his reputed homosexuality, was forced into hiding at the

home of the poet Luis Rosales. On 16 August he was arrested, and after two days of imprisonment was driven to the countryside near the village of Viznar. There he was executed by firing squad. His body was never found.

Lorca's books of poetry include *Books of Poems* (1921), *First Songs* (1927), *Songs* (1927), *Gypsy Ballads* (1928) and *Poem of Deep Song* (1931).

His plays include *The Butterfly's Evil Spell* (1920), *Mariana Pineda* (1927), *The Shoemaker's Wonderful Wife* (1930), *Blood Wedding* (1933), *The Love of Don Perlimpin* (1933), *Yerma* (1934), *When Five Years Pass* (1936) and *The House of Bernarda Alba* (1936).

Ted Hughes was born in 1930. He published numerous collections of poems and books for adults and children. His involvement in adaptations for the stage began in 1968 with a version of Seneca's *Oedipus*, first performed at the Old Vic Theatre, London. In 1971–72 he worked with Peter Brook at his International Centre for Theatre Research in Paris.

This version of Lorca's *Blood Wedding* was first performed at the Young Vic Theatre in 1996. In 1998 the Almeida Theatre produced his version of Racine's *Phèdre* and in 1999 his *Oresteia* was first performed at the National Theatre. His final work, *Alcestis*, first toured in a production by Northern Broadsides in 2000.

Ted Hughes was appointed Poet Laureate in 1984. He won the Whitbread Book of the Year in consecutive years for his two last collections of poems, *Tales from Ovid* (1997) and *Birthday Letters* (1998). He was awarded the Order of Merit in 1998, the year in which he died.

FEDERICO GARCÍA LORCA

Blood Wedding
(Bodas de Sangre)

In a new version
by Ted Hughes

faber and faber

Faber and Faber, Inc.
An affiliate of Farrar, Straus and Giroux
19 Union Square West, New York 10003

First published in 1996
by Faber and Faber Limited
3 Queen Square London WC1N 3AU

Photoset by Parker Typesetting Service, Leicester
Printed in the United States of America

A CIP record for this book
is available from the British Library

ISBN-13: 978-0-571-19006-5
ISBN-10: 0-571-19006-5

www.fsgbooks.com

US printing 10 9

Blood Wedding was first performed at the Young Vic
Theatre on 20 September 1996 with the following cast in
order of appearance:

The Bridegroom Hamish McColl
The Mother Gillian Barge
The Neighbour Polly Hemingway
The Wife Selma Alispahic
The Mother-in-Law Ruth Posner
Leonardo Jasper Britton
The Servant Polly Hemingway
The Father Sidney Livingstone
The Bride Alexandra Gilbreath
The Moon Selma Alispahic
Death as Beggar Woman Gillian Barge
Youths/Woodcutters (*in alphabetical order*)
Daniel Bennett, Jonathan Corsie, Oliver Grig
Young Women/Girls (*in alphabetical order*)
Polly Findlay, Cassie Lloyd, Rosie Tomkins

Act One

SCENE ONE

Bridegroom's home.

Bridegroom Mother.

Mother Yes.

Bridegroom I'm away now.

Mother Where are you going?

Bridegroom The vineyard.

Mother Wait a minute.

Bridegroom What is it?

Mother Take something to eat.

Bridegroom Leave it mother. I'll eat grapes. Give me the knife.

Mother The knife?

Bridegroom To cut the grapes.

Mother The knife, the knife! Damn the knife, damn all knives, damn the devil who created knives.

Bridegroom Enough of that, mother.

Mother And guns and pistols, even the tiniest little knife, even pitchforks and mattocks.

Bridegroom Yes, yes.

Mother Anything that can pierce and cut a man's body. A glorious man, an angel, his mouth like a flower, who goes out to his vines or his olives, to look after them, to care for them because they are his passed down to him from his fathers –

Bridegroom Mother, that's enough.

Mother And he never comes back. Or he comes back only to be laid out with a palm leaf over him and a plateful of rough salt to stop him swelling in the heat. How can you carry that knife on you? Why do I keep that snake in the kitchen?

Bridegroom Have you finished?

Mother If I live another hundred years I shall never be finished. First your father, fresh as a carnation, and I had him for three short years. Then your brother. How is it that something as small as a pistol or a knife can do away with a man who is like a bull? I shall never be quiet. The months pass and the despair makes my eyes raw, it makes my hair harsh –

Bridegroom Shall we stop now, mother?

Mother No, I shall not stop. Who's going to bring your father back? And your brother? And there's the prison. What is a prison? They eat in there, they smoke, they make their music. My dead are under the weeds, they can't speak, they're dust – two men who were like two beautiful blossoms, and their murderers in prison, taking their ease, gazing at the hills.

Bridegroom Would you like me to kill them?

Mother No. But I have to speak. How can I not speak, seeing you go out through that door. It's just that I don't like to see you with a knife. I don't want you to go to the fields.

Bridegroom You are being silly, mother.

Mother I wish you were a girl. Then you wouldn't be

2

going down to the stream. We'd be embroidering borders, with flowers and little woollen dogs.

Bridegroom Mother, how if I take you with me down to the vineyard?

Mother What good is an old woman in a vineyard? Maybe you could put me under the roots.

Bridegroom (*picking her up, swinging her round*) Old woman, old woman, you poor old woman.

Mother Yes, your father took me there. Good strong stock, he was. Good blood. And your grandfather left a son in every corner. That's how it should be – wheat, wheat and men, men.

Bridegroom And me. What about me?

Mother What about you?

Bridegroom Do I need to say it again?

Mother Ah.

Bridegroom You think it's a bad idea?

Mother No.

Bridegroom So?

Mother I don't know what I think. Whenever you bring it up like this, so sudden, it always gives me a shock. I know she's a good girl. Isn't she? Modest. Hardworking. She bakes the bread and makes her own clothes. But I don't know how it is. Whenever I speak her name it's as if a stone hit me between the eyes.

Bridegroom Nonsense.

Mother Is it nonsense? I shall be left alone. You are all I have now and you're going.

Bridegroom But you will come with us.

Mother No, I can't leave your father and brother! I visit them every morning. If I were to leave, and one of that Felix lot were to die, one of that gang of killers, and they were to bury him next to mine – I could never bear it. No! It must never be let happen. I'll dig them up with my bare hands and I'll smash them against the wall.

Bridegroom Don't get back into that!

Mother I'm sorry. How long have you known her?

Bridegroom Three years. And now I've bought the vineyard.

Mother Three years. Didn't she have somebody else at some time?

Bridegroom I don't know. I don't think so. A girl has to look hard before she says yes.

Mother Yes, I looked hard at your father: nobody else. And when the Felixes murdered him I just went on staring at the wall. One woman, one man and that's it.

Bridegroom You know my girl is good.

Mother I've no doubt. Even so, I'd like to know what her mother was like.

Bridegroom What would that tell you?

Mother Ah, son.

Bridegroom What are you trying to say?

Mother It's true – you're right. When shall I speak to her father?

Bridegroom Sunday?

Mother I'll take her the brass ear-rings. My old heirlooms. And you can buy her –

Bridegroom What?

Mother Some embroidered stockings. And for yourself – two suits. No, three suits. You are all I have.

Bridegroom I'm going. I shall see her tomorrow.

Mother Yes, yes. And make me happy with six grandchildren, or as many as you like – since your father couldn't give them to me.

Bridegroom Mother, the first will be for you.

Mother Yes – but remember, girls. So we can all sew and make lace and be peaceful.

Bridegroom I know you will love her.

Mother I'm sure I will. (*Makes to kiss him but desists.*) Be off. You're too big now for kisses. Give them to your wife, when she is your wife.

Bridegroom I'm away now.

Mother Work that ground by the little mill. You've been neglecting it.

Bridegroom So it's decided.

Mother God bless.

Bridegroom exits. Enter Neighbour.

Neighbour How are you?

Mother As you see.

Neighbour I came down to the shop, so thought I'd come over to see how you are. We live so far apart.

Mother I haven't been to the top of the street in twenty years.

Neighbour Perhaps you're right.

5

Mother You think so?

Neighbour Such things happen. Two days ago they brought in my neighbour's son with both his arms gone. The machine had sliced them off.

Mother Rafael?

Neighbour Yes. And now what's he good for? Often I think your son and my son are better where they are, sleeping, resting, safe from being made useless.

Mother Enough of that. Fancy thoughts can't help. There's no mending what's happened.

Neighbour Aye!

Mother Aye!

Neighbour And your son?

Mother He's just gone out.

Neighbour He bought the vineyard at last?

Mother He was lucky.

Neighbour So now he'll be getting married.

Mother Tell me something.

Neighbour Go on.

Mother Do you know this girl my son's chosen?

Neighbour A fine young woman.

Mother Yes, but –

Neighbour Nobody knows her well. She lives away out there, alone with her father – miles from the nearest house. But she's used to loneliness. She's good – a fine young woman.

Mother What about her mother?

Neighbour I knew her. A handsome woman. Her face glowed, like a saint's. But I didn't like her. She never loved her husband.

Mother The things people pick up!

Neighbour I'm sorry. Don't be offended. It's no more than the truth. Now as for her being respectable – nothing was ever said. No one ever spoke about that. She was very proud.

Mother Always the same!

Neighbour You did ask.

Mother I wish nobody had ever heard of either of them – the living one or the dead. I wish they were two thistles out there, that nobody ever came near, that would spike whoever did.

Neighbour You are right. A son is precious.

Mother So I look after mine. I heard she once had an admirer.

Neighbour When she was about fifteen. He got married two years ago. To her cousin as a matter of fact. Nobody remembers.

Mother You remember.

Neighbour You ask such questions.

Mother We're all curious about what might hurt us. Who was he?

Neighbour Leonardo.

Mother Which Leonardo?

Neighbour Leonardo Felix.

Mother Felix!

Neighbour You can't blame Leonardo for those things. He was only eight when they happened.

Mother I know it. But I hear that name Felix – and my mouth fills with mud. I have to spit – I have to spit – or I shall have to kill.

Neighbour Be calm. What's the good of this?

Mother None. But you understand it.

Neighbour Don't set yourself against your son's happiness. Tell him nothing. You're old. And I'm old. We should keep our mouths shut.

Mother I shall say nothing.

Neighbour Nothing.

Mother Things!

Neighbour I have to go. The men will be back from the fields soon.

Mother Did you ever know such heat!

Neighbour The children are worn out taking water to the harvesters. God bless you.

Mother Yes, God bless.

SCENE TWO

Leonardo's house.

Mother-in-law
   Hush, baby, hush.
   Sing of the great horse
   That wouldn't drink the water.
   The water ran black
   Under the boughs.

8

Under the bridge
It stopped and sang.
Who knows, my darling,
The pain of the water
That draws its long tail
Through long green rooms

Wife
Sleep, my blossom,
The horse will not drink.

Mother-in-law
Sleep, little rose,
The horse is weeping,
Its hooves are hurt,
Its mane is frozen.
And in its eye
A dagger of silver.
Down by the river,
Down by the river,
Blood is pouring
Stronger than the water.

Wife
Sleep, my blossom,
The horse will not drink.

Mother-in-law
Sleep, little rose,
The horse is weeping.

Wife
He will not touch
The edge of the river
He will not, he will not
Quench his muzzle
In the fringe of the river
Though it sweats

9

Flies of silver.
He can only whinny
To the hard mountains
From the dry river
Dead in his throat.
Aye, the great horse
That will not drink the water.
The sorrow of the snows,
The horse of dawn.

Mother-in-law
Keep away, stay
Close to the window
With a branch of dreams
And a dream of branches.

Wife
Now my baby sleeps.

Mother-in-law
Now my baby rests.

Wife
Horse, my baby
Has a soft pillow.

Mother-in-law
A cot of iron.

Wife
A cover of linen.

Mother-in-law
Hush, baby, hush.

Wife
Aye, the great horse
Will not drink the water.

Mother-in-law
　　Keep away, stay,
　　Run to the mountain
　　And the dark valley
　　Of the mare

Wife
　　Now my baby sleeps.

Mother-in-law
　　Now he can rest.

Wife
　　Sleep, my blossom,
　　The horse will not drink.

Mother-in-law
　　Sleep, little rose,
　　The horse is weeping.

　　They take the sleeping child in. Enter Leonardo.

Leonardo　Where's the baby?

Wife　Sleeping.

Leonardo　He wasn't right yesterday. He cried all night.

Wife　He's as fresh as a dahlia today. And you? Did you go to the blacksmith?

Leonardo　That's where I've come from. But I can't believe it. For two months I've been putting new shoes on that horse – and he's forever ripping them off. It must be the way he goes on the stones.

Wife　Maybe you're pushing him too hard.

Leonardo　I almost never use him.

Wife　Yesterday I heard you were away over the other side of the plain. People saw you.

Leonardo Who said that?

Wife The women who gather capers. I was surprised to hear it, I must say. Was it you?

Leonardo No. What would I be doing out there, in that desert?

Wife That's what I told them. But the horse came home in a lather.

Leonardo You saw him, did you?

Wife My mother saw him.

Leonardo Is she with the baby?

Wife Yes. Would you like a drink of lemon?

Leonardo Make it icy cold.

Wife I'd cooked a meal for you.

Leonardo I was down getting the wheat weighed. They always hold you up.

Wife Good price?

Leonardo Fair.

Wife I need a dress. And I want to get the baby a cap with ribbons.

Leonardo I'm going in to see him.

Wife Be quiet, he's asleep.

  Enter Mother-in-law.

Mother-in-law Who's trying to kill that horse? He's down there stretched out, with his eyeballs bulging, heaving as if he'd just come back from the end of the world.

Leonardo Me.

Mother-in-law I beg your pardon. He's your horse.

Wife He's been down at the weighing station.

Mother-in-law He can burst for all I care.

Wife Your drink. Is it cold enough?

Leonardo Thank you.

Wife Do you know my cousin's getting engaged?

Leonardo When?

Wife Tomorrow. The wedding will be less than a month. They'll invite us, I hope.

Leonardo Who knows?

Mother-in-law Well, I've heard his mother isn't so happy about it.

Leonardo She might be right. That girl has depths.

Wife You won't make me think badly about a girl as good as she is.

Mother-in-law He says what he knows. And for three years he knew her well enough, before he knew you.

Leonardo And then I left her. Are you going to cry now? Stop it. Come on, let's look at the baby.

They go out. Enter a girl.

Girl Senora?

Mother-in-law What is it?

Girl The man who's going to be married came to the shop and he bought all the best things, all the most expensive.

Mother-in-law On his own?

Girl No, with his mother. Tall, stern woman. But the things they bought!

Mother-in-law They have the money.

Girl They bought those embroidered stockings! Such embroidery! The sort you dream about. A swallow here. A boat here. And here – a rose.

Mother-in-law Child!

Girl The rose had its seeds and its stalk! Ay! All in pure silk.

Mother-in-law A marriage of two fortunes.

Enter Leonardo and Wife.

Girl You should see what your cousin's fiancé is buying at the shop. I came to tell you.

Leonardo What makes you think we want to know that?

Wife Leonardo!

Mother-in-law Was that necessary?

Girl Oh! (*Exits crying.*)

Mother-in-law Do you have to be so offensive?

Leonardo I don't need your remarks.

Mother-in-law Ah! Very good.

Wife What's wrong with you? What's going on in your head? Tell me. Don't just leave me to guess –

Leonardo That's enough.

Wife No. Look straight into my eyes and tell me.

Leonardo Leave me alone.

Wife Where are you going?

Leonardo Can't you just shut up?

Mother-in-law Be quiet! (*Leonardo leaves.*) The baby!

Wife
His hooves are hurt.
His mane is frozen.
And in his eye
A dagger of silver.
Down by the river,
Down by the river,
Blood is pouring
Stronger than the water.

Sleep, my blossom,
The horse will not drink.

Mother-in-law
Sleep, little rose,
The horse is weeping.

Wife
Sleep, child, sleep.

Mother-in-law
Ay, the great horse
That will not drink

Wife
Sleep, little rose,
The horse is weeping.

SCENE THREE

Bride's House.

Maid Please come in. Will you have a seat? They'll be with you in a moment.

Mother Are you wearing your watch?

Son Yes.

Mother We must get away in good time. This place is so far out.

Son It's good land.

Mother Yes. But too isolated. Four hours to get here and not a house or a tree.

Son It's dry country.

Mother Your father would have had it covered with trees.

Son Without water?

Mother He'd have found water. In our three years he planted ten cherry trees. The three walnuts by the mill. A whole vineyard. And a thing called a Jupiter plant with red flowers. But that dried up.

Son She must be getting herself ready.

Enter her father.

Father How long did it take you to get here?

Mother Four hours.

Father You must have come the long way round.

Mother I'm too old for all that scrambling up and down by the river.

Son It makes her sick.

Father A good crop of alfalfa.

Son Excellent.

Father At one time this land wouldn't even grow alfalfa. You have to punish it, torture it, to get anything!

Mother Now it gives plenty. But don't worry. I'm not here to beg.

Father You're far better off than I am. Your vineyards must be worth a fortune. Every sprig a coin of silver. It's a pity our farms are – well – so far apart. I like everything in one big piece. Do you know there's a little orchard right in the middle of my fields, and it's a thorn in my heart. All the gold in the world wouldn't bring them to part with it.

Son There's always something.

Father Now if you could yoke twenty pair of oxen and just drag your vineyard up here onto my hillside – think of it!

Mother What would be the point of that?

Father To see it all joined up. Yes? Mine is hers and yours is his. What a beautiful thing it would be, all joined up!

Son Less work for sure.

Mother When I'm dead you can sell ours and buy out here.

Father Sell? You never want to sell. Buy, woman, buy all you can. If I'd had sons I would have bought everything between the mountains and the stream. It's not great land but good strong shoulders can make it good enough. And since nobody ever comes near they don't steal your fruit and you can sleep easy.

Mother You know why I'm here?

Father Yes.

Mother So?

Father I see nothing wrong. And they've talked it over.

Mother My son is well set up. And he's a worker.

Father My daughter the same.

Mother My son is handsome. He has never known a woman. His name is as clean as a sheet in the sun.

Father What can I say about mine? She's up at three, with the morning star, baking bread. Never chatters. Gentle as fleece. Does all kinds of embroidery, and she can cut a rope with her teeth.

Mother God bless this house.

Father God bless it.

Servant enters with two trays: one with glasses, the other with sweets.

Mother When would you like the wedding?

Son Next Thursday.

Father That's her twenty-second birthday.

Mother Twenty-two! That's what my eldest son would have been, if he'd lived. He would be here now, warm and living, the real man he was, if knives had never been invented.

Father Don't dwell on it.

Mother My hand on my heart, not a moment passes.

Father Thursday, then. Yes.

Son Thursday it is.

Father From here, the church is quite a way. So we'll go with the bride and groom in a car. Everybody else can make do in carts or on horseback or whatever.

Mother Very good.

Servant crosses room.

Father Tell her to come in. I shall be a very happy man if you like her.

Bride enters.

Mother Come here, my child. Are you happy?

Bride Yes, senora.

Father Don't be so solemn. After all, she's going to be your mother.

Bride I'm happy. When I say 'yes', I say it because I mean it.

Mother Of course. Look at me.

Father She's my wife all over again.

Mother Is she? Such a beautiful look! You know what marriage means, my child?

Bride I do.

Mother A man, children, and for everybody else a wall two feet thick.

Son Who needs more?

Mother Life – that's what they need more than anything else – life.

Bride I know my duty.

Mother Here are some small gifts.

Bride Thank you.

Father A little something?

Mother Not for me. (*to son*) Have something.

Son I will.

Father Wine.

Mother He never touches it.

Father All the better!

Son I'll come tomorrow.

Bride What time?

Son Five o'clock.

Bride I shall expect you.

Son Whenever I leave you I feel a great emptiness and a kind of lump in my throat.

Bride Once you're my husband that will go.

Son So I tell myself.

Mother Let's be off. The sun won't wait. Is everything agreed?

Father Everything.

Mother (*to servant*) Goodbye.

Servant God be with you.

(*Mother kisses the bride.*)

Mother Goodbye daughter.

Exit Mother and son.

Father I'll see you on your way.

Servant Oh let's look at the presents, I can't wait.

Bride Stop that.

Servant Let's just take a peep at them.

Bride I don't want to.

Servant Just the stockings. They say it's the most intricate work from top to bottom.

Bride No.

Servant For God's sake. We'll not touch them then. It's as if you didn't want to get married.

Bride (*biting her hand in anger*) Ah!

Servant Girl, girl, what's the matter? Can't you bear to give up this queenly life of yours? You mustn't think painful thoughts. You have no reason to. None whatsoever. Let's look at the presents. (*Picks up the box.*)

Bride (*gripping her wrists*) Let go.

Servant Aaah!

Bride I said let go.

Servant You're stronger than a man.

Bride Because I've always done a man's work? I wish I were a man.

Servant Stop talking like this.

Bride Yes, let's stop it. Let's talk about something else.

Servant Did you hear a horse last night?

Bride Last night? What time?

Servant About three.

Bride A stray, probably.

Servant No. It was being ridden.

Bride How do you know?

Servant I saw the rider. He came to your window. It gave me a shock.

Bride Wasn't it my fiancé? He's been here before at that time.

Servant No.

Bride You saw him?

Servant Yes.

Bride Who was it?

Servant Leonardo.

Bride You're lying. You're lying. What would he be doing here?

Servant I saw him.

Bride Shut up. A curse on your tongue!

Horse's hooves heard.

Servant Come here, look. Was it him?

Bride It was him.

Act Two

SCENE ONE

Bride's house, entrance.

Servant Oh, this heat!

Bride Finish doing my hair out here. The house is much too hot.

Servant We don't even get that moment at dawn when everything cools and the air stirs a little.

Bride sits. Servant combs.

Bride My mother came from rich country, full of trees.

Servant So she was full of life.

Bride And here she withered away.

Servant It was her Fate!

Bride Like we're all withering away. A flame comes off these walls. Ow, don't pull so hard.

Servant I'm trying to get this bit of hair right. I want it down over your forehead, like that (*Bride looks in mirror.*) Oh, you're so beautiful! (*Kisses her impulsively.*)

Bride Just finish combing my hair.

Servant (*combing*) You are so lucky! To wrap your arms around a man, to kiss him, to feel his weight.

Bride That's enough.

Servant And the best moment of all, when you wake up and feel him beside you, his breath stroking your shoulder – like a nightingale's feather –

23

Bride Please will you shut up.

Servant But child! What is marriage? That's what marriage is – nothing else. Is it all the cakes, the sweets, the dainties? Is it the bouquets of flowers. No. It's a shining white bed. And a woman. And a man.

Bride You shouldn't talk about it.

Servant No? But that's what it's all about. Think of it – that endless pleasure.

Bride Or endless bitterness.

Servant If I fix the orange blossom from here to here, it will make a crown. (*Ties the orange blossom.*)

Bride Let me have it.

*Looks in mirror, takes orange blossom, lowers her head
dejectedly.*

Servant What is the matter?

Bride Leave me alone.

Servant This is no time for dark thoughts. Give me the orange blossom.

Bride flings the blossoms aside.

Child! Flinging you wedding wreath away! Are you trying to tempt Fate? Here – look into my eyes. Do you want to get married or not? Say it. There is still time.

Bride Black clouds. An icy wind blowing, here, deep inside. Does everybody feel this?

Servant Do you love this man you're going to marry?

Bride I love him, yes, I love him.

Servant Yes, yes, you love him.

Bride But it's such a huge step.

Servant It has to be taken.

Bride And I have already promised.

Servant Let me fix the wreath.

Bride Hurry. They'll start arriving any moment.

Servant They'll have been on the road two hours at least.

Bride How far from here to the church?

Servant Two hours if you cross the river. Twice as far if you go by the road.

Bride stands, servant watches.

Servant
Let the bride awake
On the morning of her wedding.
Let all the rivers of the world
Bear her flowering wreath.

Bride (*smiling*) Let's go.

Servant (*dancing around her*)
Let her awaken
With the green branch
Of the flowering laurel.
Let her awaken
With the trunk and the branch
Of the laurel flowers.

Loud knocking.

Bride That must be the first guest. It's still dark. Open the door.

Bride goes in. Servant opens door.

Servant You!

Leonardo Yes, me. Good morning.

Servant You're the first!

Leonardo Wasn't I invited?

Servant Of course.

Leonardo So here I am.

Servant And your wife?

Leonardo I came on horseback. She's coming the long way round.

Servant Didn't you meet anybody else.

Leonardo I passed a few.

Servant You're going to kill that horse.

Leonardo When he's dead he's dead.

Servant Take a seat. Nobody's up yet.

Leonardo Not the bride?

Servant I'm going in now to dress her.

Leonardo The bride! I expect she's feeling happy.

Servant And the baby?

Leonardo Baby?

Servant Your son.

Leonardo (*remembering, as in a dream*) Ah!

Servant Will he be coming?

Leonardo No.

   Pause. Singing in distance.

Voices
   Let the bride awake

On the morning of her wedding.

Leonardo
  Let the bride awake
  On the morning of her wedding.

Servant Here they come now. Still a good way off.

Leonardo (*getting up*) I expect she will be wearing a big wreath. It shouldn't be too big. Something quite small would suit her best. And did the groom bring her the orange blossom – to go over her heart?

Bride (*she appears in petticoats, with the wreath fixed in place*) Yes, he brought it.

Servant Don't come out like that, half-dressed.

Bride What difference does it make? Why do you want to know whether he brought the orange blossom? What are you insinuating?

Leonardo Nothing. Why should I? (*Moves closer.*) You know me, you know I say what I think. Tell me, what was I to you? Dig in your memory, open it up. A couple of oxen and a rough shack are almost nothing. That's what hurts.

Bride Why have you come?

Leonardo To watch your wedding.

Bride As I watched yours.

Leonardo You forced me into that, you tied that knot with your own two hands. They can kill me but they can't spit on me, with all their silver.

Bride I never forced you.

Leonardo I don't want to raise my voice. I am a man of honour. I don't want all these hills hearing my complaints.

27

Bride Mine would be louder.

Servant Will you stop this. Don't rake up the past. Let it go.

Servant watches the doors anxiously.

Bride She's right. I shouldn't be talking to you. But my blood boils to see how you've come here today to spy on my wedding and make evil insinuations about the orange blossom. Get out. Go and wait for your wife outside.

Leonardo Can't you and I even talk?

Servant No, you cannot.

Leonardo Ever since my own wedding day I've been asking myself night and day who was to blame. And I'm always finding somebody new to blame. – Because somebody somewhere must be to blame.

Bride A man with a horse knows plenty and can do plenty to run rings round a girl stuck in the middle of a desert. But I have my pride. And so now, I am getting married. I shall shut myself away with my husband and love him alone, above everybody and everything else.

Leonardo (*approaching her*) Your pride won't save you.

Bride Don't come near me.

Leonardo We cannot punish ourselves worse than to burn and stay silent. What good did my pride do me – not seeing you, and knowing you were lying awake night after night. None! It only poured blazing coals over me. You think time heals and that walls shut away but it's not true, it's not true. When things have pierced to the centre nobody can pull them out.

Bride (*trembling*) I daren't listen to you. I daren't hear your voice. It's as if I'd drunk a bottle of anise and fallen

28

asleep on a great heap of lilies. It drags me, I know I'm drowning, and I'm helpless.

Servant (*taking Leonardo by the lapels*) Go. You must go. Now. Go.

Leonardo What's the matter? This is the last time I shall ever speak to her.

Bride I know I'm mad, I know my heart's ground to dust with holding out, but I can't help myself – I hear his voice, I see his arms moving, and I can't –

Leonardo I shall never be at peace unless I tell you these things. I got married. Now you get married.

Servant She will. That's one thing you can be sure of.

Voices
    Let the bride awake
    On the morning of her wedding.

Bride
    Let the bride awake.

She runs out.

Servant Here are the guests. (*to Leonardo*) Don't come near her again.

Leonardo You needn't worry.

He goes. It starts to get light.

First Girl
    Let the bride awake
    On the morning of her wedding.
    Start dancing in a ring,
    Hang flower wreaths
    From every window.

Voices
    Let the bride awake.

Servant
    Let her wake up
    With the green branch
    Of flowering laurel.
    Let her wake up
    With the trunk and the branch
    Of the laurel flowers.

Second Girl
    Let her awaken,
    Her long hair loose,
    Her bodice of snow.
    And over her brow,
    Flowers of jasmine.

Servant
    Ay, farmer's daughter,
    See the moon climb.

First Girl
    Ay, young man,
    Leave your broad hat
    On the bough of the olive.

First Youth
    Let the bride awaken.
    The wedding guests are coming
    Across the far fields
    With baskets of dahlias,
    With loaves that are blest.

Voices
    Let the bride awaken.

Second Girl
    The bride, the bride

Puts on her white wreath.
The groom, the groom
Ties it with gold ribbons.

Servant
By the grapefruit tree
The bride will lie awake.

Third Girl
By the orange tree
The groom will give her
Spoon and napkin.

Three Guests enter.

First Girl
O dove, awake,
The dawn is brightening
The bells of darkness.

Guest
The bride, the white bride,
Today she's a maiden,
Tomorrow a woman.

First Girl
Come down, dark one,
Dragging your train of silk.

Guest
Come down, little dark one,
The morning dew is icy.

First Youth
Awake, bride, awake.
Let the air carry
The orange blossom

Servant
I shall embroider a tree

Flowing with dark red ribbons,
With long life, with children.

Voices
Let the bride awaken.

First Youth
On the morning of her wedding.

Guest
On the morning of your wedding
How beautiful you are.
Wife worthy a warrior,
Flower of the mountain.

Father
Wife worthy a warrior,
The groom carries her off.
He is coming with oxen
To claim his prize.

Third Girl
The groom is a golden flower.
Where his foot falls
Carnations spring up.

Servant
Oh my lucky child!

Second Youth
Let the bride awaken.

Servant
A beautiful bride!

First Girl
From every window
The wedding is calling.

Second Girl
Let the bride come out.

First Girl
She's coming, she's coming!

Servant
Ring and ring again
Bells for the wedding.

First Girl
She's coming! She's here.

Servant
Now the wedding
Starts to move
Like a huge bull.

Bride appears. Guitars. Girls kiss the bride.

Third Girl What's that perfume you've put on your hair?

Bride I haven't put any.

Second Girl What's this material? I never saw anything like it.

First Youth Here's the groom.

Bridegroom Greetings.

First Girl
The bridegroom
Is a golden flower

Second Girl
The joy in his eyes
Makes our eyes joyful.

Groom goes to bride.

Bridegroom What made you choose those shoes for today?

Bride They're not so gloomy as the black ones.

Leonardo's Wife (*enters and kisses the bride*) Blessings on you both.

Everybody chatters.

Leonardo (*stiffly*)
  The morning of your wedding
  You must wear this wreath.

Leonardo's Wife
  So the dew of your hair
  Will make the fields happy.

Groom's Mother (*to Bride's Father*) What are they doing here?

Father They are family. Today is a day of forgiveness.

Mother I may bear it but I don't forgive it.

Bridegroom It's wonder just to look at you in that crown.

Bride Can't we go straight to the church now?

Bridegroom In such a hurry?

Bride Yes, I am. I want to be your wife and alone with you, hearing no voice but yours.

Bridegroom I want that too.

Bride I want to see no eyes but yours. And I want you to hold me so hard and strong that even if my mother called to me, my dead mother, I couldn't pull free.

Bridegroom My arms are strong. They're going to hold you tight for forty years.

Bride Forever! Never let me go.

Father Let's be off. Get into the carts, get up on the horses. The sun has risen.

Mother O tread carefully. We don't want any bad omens.

All begin to leave.

Servant
When you go from your home,
O white girl,
Remember you go
Like a shooting star.

First Girl
Your body new
As your wedding dress,
You go from your home
To your wedding.

Second Girl
You go from your home
To the church.

Servant
The wind strews petals
Over the sand.

Third Girl
Oh, the white girl.

Servant
A dark wind
Lifts the lace
Of her mantilla.

They leave. Guitars. Music. Leonardo and his Wife remain.

Wife Are we going?

Leonardo Where?

Wife The church. But not on horseback. You come with me.

Leonardo In the cart?

Wife What's the alternative?

Leonardo I'm not the kind of man who goes anywhere in a cart.

Wife And I'm not the kind of woman who goes to a wedding without her husband. I can't stand any more of this.

Leonardo Nor can I.

Wife Don't look at me like that. Your eyes are two thorns.

Leonardo Why don't we just go.

Wife What's happening to us? I think and I don't want to think. But I'm certain of one thing. You have already thrown me away. I have a child. And another is coming. That's how it is. It happened to my mother, and now it is happening to me. But you're not moving me from here.

Voices
    When you go from your home
    To the church,
    Remember you go
    Like a shooting star.

Wife (*weeping*)
    Remember you go
    Like a star.
That's how I went from my home too. I thought I'd been given the whole world.

Leonardo Let's go.

Wife Together?

Leonardo As you wish. Come.

    When you go from your home
    To the church,
    Remember you go
    Like a shooting star.

SCENE TWO

Outside the bride's farm-house. Servant arranging glasses and trays on a table.

Servant
    Turning, the wheel
    Was turning. The water
    Was pouring by.
    For the wedding night
    Let the bending moon
    Part the dark branches
    And look down
    From her white balcony.

    (*loud*) Spread the tablecloths.

    Singing, the bride
    And the groom were singing.
    The water went swiftly.
    For the wedding night
    Let the frost blaze,
    Let the bitter almond
    Be sweet as honey.

    (*loud*) Open the wine.

    Loveliest, O girl
    Loveliest on earth,
    See the water flowing
    Your wedding night is near.
    Tighten your skirt, hide
    Under your husband's wing.
    Never leave the house.
    Your husband is a dove
    Whose breast burns.
    The fields wait for the cry
    Of blood escaping.

Turning, the wheel
Was turning. The water
Was pouring by.
This is your wedding night.
The water is flaming.

Mother (*entering*) At last!

Father Are we the first?

Servant No. Leonardo and his wife got back a while ago.
They drove like demons. His poor wife was half dead with
fright. He made that cart go like a horse with one rider.

Father That boy will come to a bad end. The blood's no
good.

Mother How could it be good? His whole tribe is rotten.
The great grandfather began it – he started the murders.
Now we have a whole family of smiles wrapped around
daggers.

Father We should drop this now.

Servant How can she drop it?

Mother Every vein in my body aches with it. In every face
in that family I see nothing but the face that murdered
mine. Look at me. Do I seem crazy? I am crazy, with
everything I've had to hold down and hold in, everything
that my heart wants to scream out. There's a great scream
always fighting its way up. I have to smother it and shove
it back down. I have to suffocate it in these shawls.
They've taken my dead ones and I have to be dumb. And
then people talk about me. (*Removes her shawl.*)

Father It's not the day to be dwelling on this.

Mother Once I start, I have to say what I have to say.
Today more than ever. Today I'm left absolutely alone.

38

Father But with one great hope – of new company.

Mother The one hope left: grandchildren.

Father The more the better. This land needs strong hands that cost nothing. It's a perpetual battle – against weeds, against thistles, against stones that just come up out of nowhere. Only men who own the land will dominate it and punish it hard enough to make the seed spring. We need many sons.

Mother Daughters also. Men are too like the wind. They live in a world of weapons. At least girls keep off the streets.

Father I think they'll have plenty of both.

Mother As bulls go, my son will be a good worker. Good seed. His father could have sired many children on me.

Father If only they could get it all done in one day. Suddenly – two or three sons, grown men.

Mother It's not the way it happens, is it. A slow, long business. So it is terrible – when you see that blood emptied into the ground. A fountain that leaps for a few seconds – and it cost you all those years. When I got to my son he was lying in the middle of the street. I put my hands in his blood and licked them. Because it was me, mine. You don't understand that. I would have kept that blood-soaked dirt in a chalice of glass and topaz.

Father But now we have something to hope for. My daughter has wide hips, your son has a strong back.

Mother Yes, a hope.

Father Are the trays of wheat ready?

Servant They're ready.

Leonardo's Wife (*entering*) I hope they will be very happy.

39

Mother Thank you.

Leonardo Is there going to be music and dancing?

Father Not for long. People have to be away.

Servant Here they are.

Enter Guests and Bridal couple, Leonardo leaves.

Bridegroom Was there ever a wedding with so many people!

Bride Never!

Father It was magnificent!

Mother Whole families are here.

Bridegroom Some who never step out of the house.

Mother Your father sowed and now you reap.

Bridegroom I've met cousins I never knew existed.

Mother All those people from the coast.

Bridegroom The horses scared them.

Mother (*to Bride*) You're thoughtful.

Bride Me? Not at all.

Guitars.

Mother So many blessings – they can weigh heavy.

Bride Like lead.

Mother Don't let them. Today you should be light as a dove.

Bride Will you stay here tonight?

Mother No. My house is empty.

Bride Then stay with us.

Father (*to Mother*) Look at the dance they're starting. That's a dance from the coast.

Leonardo enters and sits. His wife stands behind him.

Mother My husband's cousins. They're tireless dancers, they'll wear out the stones.

Father It's wonderful to see them. Just what this house needs. (*He leaves.*)

Bridegroom (*to Bride*) You liked the orange-blossom?

Bride (*looking at him fixedly*) Yes.

Bridegroom It's made of wax. It will last forever. I would have liked to see your dress covered with it.

Bride No need for that.

Leonardo goes off.

First Girl Shall we take your pins out?

Bride (*to Bridegroom*) I'll be back in a moment.

Leonardo's Wife I hope you will be happy with my cousin.

Bridegroom I'm sure I shall.

Wife Just the two of you here together. Never going out, building a home. If only we lived as far away from everything as this.

Bridegroom Buy some land here. The mountain's cheap. And it's an excellent place for bringing up children.

Wife We don't have the money! And the way we're going –

Bridegroom Your husband is a good worker.

Wife Yes, but he flits about too much! All over the place. He's a restless man.

Servant Aren't you going to eat something? I'll wrap up some wine-cakes for your mother. I know she loves them.

Bridegroom Get her three dozen.

Wife No, no. Just a few will be plenty.

Bridegroom This is a special day.

Wife (*to Servant*) Where is Leonardo?

Servant I haven't seen him.

Bridegroom He'll be out there with the guests.

Wife I didn't see him (*She goes out.*)

Servant That is nice.

Bridegroom Why aren't you dancing?

Servant Nobody wants to dance with me.

Bridegroom They don't understand, do they. Merry old girls like you dance far better than the young ladies.

Servant Are you flirting with me? Your whole family's the same. Men among men. I can remember your grandfather's wedding. What a man he was! Like a mountain there at the altar.

Bridegroom I'm built differently.

Servant But the same glint in your eye! Where's our beauty?

Bridegroom Taking off her veil and wreath.

Servant Ah, yes. I've prepared you a little something for midnight. I don't suppose you'll be sleeping. Some ham, and some big glasses of old wine. On the bottom shelf of the cupboard. You just might feel the need.

Bridegroom I don't eat at night.

Servant Your bride might be glad of it.

First Youth (*entering*) You have to drink with us.

Bridegroom I'm waiting for my wife.

Second Youth She'll be yours before dawn.

First Youth That's the best time, just before dawn.

Second Youth One drink.

Bridegroom All right.

> *They leave. Sounds of excitement. Bride appears. Two girls run to meet her.*

First Girl Who did you give the first pin to? Me or her?

Bride I don't remember.

First Girl You gave it to me – here.

Second Girl You gave it to me – in the church.

Bride (*agitated*) I don't know.

First Girl But can't you –

Bride I can't. I don't care who got it. I have so much to think about.

Second Girl I'm sorry.

Bride (*she sees Leonardo*) There is so much upset. It's a difficult time.

First Girl Is that what it's like?

Bride You'll know when the day comes for you. It's a hard step, a painful step.

First Girl Are you angry about it?

Bride Of course not. I'm sorry.

Second Girl What for? But both pins mean you'll get married, don't they?

Bride Either one, you'll get married.

First Girl But one of us will get married first.

Bride Are you in such a hurry?

Second Girl Yes.

Bride Why?

First Girl Because – (*Hugs Second Girl.*)

*Girls run out. Bridegroom enters slowly and embraces
Bride from behind.*

Bride No!

Bridegroom Do I scare you?

Bride Oh, it's you.

Bridegroom Who else? Your father?

Bride Yes.

Bridegroom Your Father wouldn't have been so rough.

Bride You're right, he wouldn't.

Bridegroom Because he's old. (*He embraces her roughly.*)

Bride Stop it!

Bridegroom Why?

Bride Because – all these people. They will see us.

(*Servant comes over, ignoring the couple.*)

Bridegroom So? We are man and wife.

Bride Yes, but let me go. Later.

Bridegroom What's the matter? You're so tense!

Bride It's nothing. Don't go.

Leonardo's Wife appears.

Wife I didn't mean to interrupt –

Bridegroom What is it?

Wife Has my husband come this way?

Bridegroom I haven't seen him.

Wife He's nowhere – and his horse has gone from the stable.

Bridegroom He'll have taken it for a gallop.

Wife goes. Servant enters.

Servant You must be giddy with all these toasts and blessings and congratulations.

Bridegroom I wish it were over. My wife is tired, I think.

Servant What's the matter, child?

Bride I feel I've been clubbed on the head.

Servant A bride from these mountains should be strong. She's yours now. It's up to you to cure her.

She runs out.

Bridegroom Let's dance.

Bride I think I must lie down.

Bridegroom I'll come with you.

Bride We can't. Not with all these people. What would they say? Just let me rest a while.

Bridegroom As you like. I hope you won't be feeling this way tonight.

Bride I'll be better by then.

Bridegroom Let's hope so.

Exit Bride. Enter Mother.

Mother Son.

Bridegroom Where have you been?

Mother In all that noise. You happy?

Bridegroom Yes.

Mother Where's your wife?

Bridegroom Having a little rest. Bad day for brides.

Mother A bad day? The only good one. For me it was like a great inheritance.

Servant enters, goes towards bride's room.

The breaking of the sod, the planting of the saplings.

Bridegroom Are you going to stay?

Mother No. I want to sleep in my own house.

Bridegroom Alone.

Mother Not alone. My head is full of things. Of men. Of fighting.

Bridegroom Fighting that is fighting no longer.

Servant enters quickly and runs off out back.

Mother While you live, you fight.

Bridegroom Whatever you say, mother.

Mother Show your wife a lot of love, and if she gets cross or moody, hug her so hard you hurt her just a little. A rough embrace and a bite – frighten her just a little. Then a soft kiss. She'll understand. It will teach her that you are the man, the boss, the one who gives the commands. I learned that from your father. You don't have him to show you how to be strong, so you must listen to me.

Bridegroom Mother, you know I will always listen to you.

Father (*entering*) Where is my daughter?

Bridegroom In her room.

First Girl Where are the bride and groom – we're going to dance the round dance.

First Youth You have to lead it.

Father (*re-entering*) She's not there.

Bridegroom Not there?

Father Perhaps she went up on the balcony.

Noise and guitars.

First Girl They're beginning (*Exit.*)

Bridegroom She's not there.

Mother Where can she have gone?

Father She must be somewhere.

Servant (*entering*) Where is she?

Mother She's disappeared.

Exit Bridegroom. Three Guests enter.

Father Isn't she dancing?

Servant No she is not dancing.

Father But there's a mass of people out there. Go and look.

Servant I've looked.

Father So where is she?

Bridegroom (*entering*) She's vanished.

Leonardo's Wife enters.

Wife They've gone. They've run away. She and Leonardo. On a horse. Like a whirlwind. Her arms around him.

Father No! Not my daughter.

Mother Yes, your daughter. Like her mother. Wicked from wicked. Gone with him. But now she's the wife of my son.

Bridegroom Let's get after them. Where's a horse?

Mother A horse! Quick! Who's got a horse. I'll give him everything I have, I'll give my eyes, my tongue.

Voice Let's go.

Mother Go. Go. Get after them. (*He goes out with two guests.*) No, don't go. That family's so ready to kill and so hardened to it – but go, yes, go. I'll follow them.

Father It can't be her. Perhaps she's thrown herself into the water-tank.

Mother Only clean, decent girls throw themselves into the water – not her kind. And now she's the wife of my son. Two families. Now there are two families dragged into it – mine and yours. Everybody must go. We must help my son. All his people are here – all you from the coast and from everywhere else. Get moving, get out on the roads, every direction, search everywhere. The bloody days are back. Both families! You with yours. Me with mine. Get after them! Get after them!

Act Three

SCENE ONE

Forest. Three Woodcutters.

First Have they found them?

Second No. But they're searching everywhere.

Third It won't take them long.

Second Shhh!

Third What?

Second They seem to be coming down every road.

First When the moon rises they'll find them.

Second They should leave them alone.

First The world's a big place. There's room for everybody.

Third You should do what you have to do. They were right to run away.

First They were deceiving themselves, but the blood couldn't be denied.

Third The blood!

First When the blood chooses a path it has to be followed.

Second But blood that sees the light is swallowed by the dust.

First So? Better be a bloodless carcase than alive with the blood rotting in your body.

Third Quiet!

First What is it? Do you hear something?

Third The crickets. The frogs. The night in ambush.

First But nowhere a horse.

Third Now they're making love.

First His body for her. Hers for him.

Second When they find them they'll kill them.

First By then they'll have poured their blood together. They'll be two empty pitchers, two dry streams.

Second With all these clouds the moon could stay hidden.

Third The Bridegroom will find them, moon or no moon. I saw him rush off. Like a raging star. His face the colour of ashes. He carried the fate of his family.

First His family dead in the street!

Second A family of dead men.

Third Do you think they'll manage to break through the cordon?

Second Not easy. There are knives and guns for ten miles in every direction.

Third His horse is good.

Second But he's carrying a woman.

First We are getting close.

Second A tree with forty branches. Soon brought down.

Third Here comes the moon. Let's hurry.

Brilliant light grows from left.

First
The moon rises.

A moon with great leaves.

Second
Fill the blood with jasmine.

First
Lonely moon.
Moon with green leaves.

Second
A wash of silver
On the face of the bride

Third
Evil moon,
Cover their love
With a shadowy branch.

First
Sorrowful moon,
Cover their love
With a branch of shadow.

*Exit Woodcutters. Enter the Moon – a young
woodcutter with a white face. Intense blue light.*

Moon
Round swan on the river,
Cathedral's eye.
And among the leaves
A false dawn –
I am all these things.
They cannot escape.
Who hides? Who weeps
In the shrubs of the valley?
The moon leaves a knife
Hanging in the sky –
An ambush of lead
That lies in wait

For the agony of blood.
Let me in! I'm freezing
On walls and windows.
Open your houses,
Open your hearts,
Let me in! Warm me.
I'm cold. My ashes
Of sleepy metal climb
To the crests of fire
On roofs, on mountains.
Snow carries me
On shoulders of jasper.
And water drowns me
Cold and hard,
In every pool.
Tonight there'll be blood
To warm my cheeks.
Let there be no shadow,
No secret corner
To keep them safe.
I want to slide
Into a bosom
Where I can be warm.
A heart for me!
Warm, spilling warm
Over the mountains
Of my breast
Let me in. Let me in.

To the branches.

I don't want shadows.
I want my beams
To pierce every cranny.
Among dark trees,
A rumour of glitters.
Tonight there'll be blood

To warm my cheeks.
Who hides? Come out.
They won't escape.
I'll make the horse flash
With a fever of diamonds.

*Moon disappears among tree-trunks. Darkness. Old
beggar woman appears in her dark green cloth. Feet
bare. Face hardly seen among the folds.*

Beggar Woman
The moon goes in and they come nearer.
Here they shall stay. The lacerated
Flight of their screams
Will be stifled
By the voice of the trees, and the voice of the river.
This is the place. This is the time.
I am tired. On bedroom floors
The coffins lie open.
The white sheets are spread
For heavy bodies
With their throats cut. And the birds
Will go on sleeping. The wind
Will bundle their cries
In her skirt and fly off with them
Over the dark trees,
Or bury them
In soft mud.
The moon! The moon!

Moon appears, with the blue light.

Moon
They're coming closer.
Some down the ravine, some along the river.
I'll light up the rocks. What do you need?

Beggar Woman
Nothing.

Moon
The wind is blowing harder, a two-edged wind.

Beggar Woman
Shine on the waistcoat, undo the buttons.
Show the knives where to go.

Moon
But let them take a long time to die.
Let the blood
Set between my fingers its delicate whistle.
Look, my valleys of ashes are coming awake,
Parched for this fountain – thirsting
For the tumbling jet of this fountain.

Beggar Woman
Shhh! They must not get beyond the stream.

Moon
There. They're coming.

Moon goes. Darknes.

Beggar Woman Quick. Light, more light! Do you hear
me. They mustn't escape.

*Enter Bridegroom and First Youth. Beggar Woman sits
and covers her face.*

Bridegroom This way.

First Youth You'll never find them.

Bridegroom I will find them.

First Youth They've gone some other way.

Bridegroom I don't think so. I heard hoofbeats just then.

First Youth There are horses all over the place tonight.

54

Bridegroom Listen. In the whole world there is only one horse, and this is it. Understand that? If you're coming with me, come, but don't talk.

First Youth I only –

Bridegroom Be quiet. I'll find them here, I know it. Look at this arm. It isn't my arm. This is my brother's arm, my father's arm, the arm of my whole dead family. And there's such strength in it, it could rip those trees out by the roots. Quick now, come on. I feel the teeth of my whole family clenched in me so I can hardly breathe.

Beggar Woman Oh!

First Youth Did you hear that?

Bridegroom You go round that way.

First Youth This is like hunting.

Bridegroom Yes, hunting. The greatest hunt of them all.

First Youth exits. Bridegroom stumbles over Beggar Woman.

Beggar Woman Oh!

Bridegroom What are you doing here?

Beggar Woman I'm cold.

Bridegroom Where are you heading?

Beggar Woman (*whining*) A long, long way.

Bridegroom Where are you from?

Beggar Woman Over there – far off.

Bridegroom Have you seen a man and a woman together on a horse, riding fast?

Beggar Woman Wait. (*as if awakening*) Such a handsome

55

young man – asleep you'd be beautiful.

Bridegroom Answer me. Have you seen them?

Beggar Woman With broad shoulders like yours – you should let them take your weight – instead of walking about on feet that are so small.

Bridegroom Did you see them? Did they come this way?

Beggar Woman (*strongly*) No, they didn't. But now they're coming. Off the mountain. Listen. You hear them?

Bridegroom I hear nothing.

Beggar Woman Do you know that path?

Bridegroom I'll try it.

Beggar Woman Let me come with you. I know my way around here.

Bridegroom Come on. Which way?

Beggar Woman That way.

They leave. Enter three Woodcutters.

First
Rising death.
Death on the big leaves.

Second
Don't broach the jet of blood.

First
Lonely death.
Death on the dry leaves.

Third
Don't bury the wedding in flowers.

Second
Sorrowful death.
Leave them a green branch.

First
Hideous death.
Leave them a green branch.

Exit as they speak. Leonardo and Bride enter.

Leonardo
Quiet!

Bride
I'll go on alone from here. You go back. Leave me.

Leonardo
Be quiet!

Bride
However you can do it,
With your hands, with your teeth,
Tear this chain from my throat.
Leave me here
Locked up in the earth.
And if you can't kill me
As you'd kill a little snake,
Then give me your gun.
Your gun in my bride's hands.
Nothing but grief,
Guilt and fire
Sweeping up through my head,
Filling my tongue
With splinters of glass.

Leonardo
Be quiet. We've taken the step.
They're close.
Where I go you go.

Bride

You'll have to force me.

Leonardo

Force you?
Who led the way down the stairs?

Bride

I did.

Leonardo

Who put a new bridle on the horse?

Bride

I did. I know.

Leonardo

Which hands fastened my spurs?

Bride

These, and they're yours.
They see you and they want
To tear the blue branches
Of your veins.
I love you! I love you!
O leave me. If I could kill you
I'd wrap you in a shroud
Edged with violet.
Nothing but grief
Grief and fire
Sweeping up through my head
Filling my tongue
With splinters of glass.

Leonardo

And my tongue, too
Stuck full of splinters
Of glass.
Because I needed to forget

And put a wall of stone
Between your house and mine.
It's the truth. Do you forget that?
When I saw you in the distance
I threw sand in my eyes.
Whenever I got astride my horse
It went straight to your door.
Then those wedding pins,
Those two silver wedding pins,
They turned my blood black.
The dream of it
Filled my whole body
With poisonous weeds.
But none of it's my fault.
It's the fault of the earth
And of that perfume
That comes off your breasts and your hair.

Bride
    Oh, there's no sense to it.
I don't want your bed or your table
But every minute of the day
I want to be with you.
You drag me with you.
You tell me to go back
And I come after you through the air
Like a leaf torn off.
I've left a faithful man
And all his family
In the middle of my wedding.
Still wearing my bride's wreath.
But it's you that will have to pay for it.
I don't want it to happen.
Leave me and go.
Nobody will defend you.

Leonardo
  The birds are waking up.
  They smell the morning.
  Night is dying
  On the edges of rocks.
  Let's find a dark place
  Where I can love you forever.
  People don't matter.
  The poisons they can pour over us
  Don't matter.

  They embrace.

Bride
  I will sleep at your feet,
  I will guard your dreams,
  Naked, looking out at the fields,
  Like a hound bitch.
  That's what I am!
  I look at you
  And your beauty burns me.

Leonardo
  Flame makes flame.
  One small flame
  Can destroy
  Two grains of corn
  Lying together.
  We must go.

  He pulls her.

Bride.
  Where will you take me?

Leonardo
  Some place these searchers
  Will never find.
  Then I'll gaze at you.

Bride

Take me to fairgrounds.
Where good honest women
Can see how shameless I am.
Where everybody
Can stare at my wedding sheets,
Like flags blowing in the wind.

Leonardo

If I thought as I should think
I would leave you too.
But where you go I go.
You too. Take a step and prove it.
Nails of moonlight
Have fastened together
My waist and your hips.

Bride

Listen.

Leonardo

They're coming.

Bride

Oh, go, go.
It's right that I should die here,
My feet in water,
My head among thorns.
The leaves can weep
For a lost woman
Who never knew a man.

Leonardo

Be quiet. They're close.

Bride

Go.

Leonardo
    Sh! They'll hear us.
    You first. Now. Listen.

Bride
    Together.

Leonardo
    As you like.
    If they can part us
    I shall be dead.

Bride
    And I shall be dead.

Exeunt, embracing.

*Moon appears, with blue light. Violins – two screams
and violins stop. Beggar Woman appears, back to
audience. Opens cloak, centre stage.*

SCENE TWO

White room. Two girls in blue, winding skein of red wool.

First Girl
    Red wool, red wool,
    What will you make?
    Red wool, red wool,
    What would you like
    To become?

Second Girl
    A dress of jasmine,
    A scarf of crystal.
    Begin at four
    But finish by ten.
    One thread of my wool

Will fetter your ankles.
Will knot and choke
The bitter wreath.

Little Girl Did you see the wedding?

First Girl No.

Little Girl
Neither did I.
O what happened
Down in the vineyard?
What happened?
In the shadow of the olives?
What's happened?
Nobody's come back.
Did you see the wedding?

Second Girl We've told you we didn't.

Little Girl (*leaving*) Neither did I.

Second Girl
Red wool, red wool, what is your song?
Red wool, red wool,
What would you like
To sing about?

First Girl
Wounds, wounds
Made of wax
And everlasting.
Sudden pain
Of a carnation
Opened by moonlight.
Days with eyes
Closed as stones.
Nights with eyes
Open under earth.

Little Girl (*in door*)
　The wool is broken
　By a sharp stone.
　A flint cut it.
　A blue, sharp mountain
　Set it free.
　It runs, it runs
　Because it must
　To break the bread.
　And bury the knife.

　Goes.

Second Girl
　Red wool, red wool,
　What are you saying.
　Red wool, red wool,
　What would you like
　To tell us?

First Girl
　The lover is speechless.
　The groom is red.
　On the bank of the river
　I saw them lying.

　She stops and looks at the wool.

Little Girl (*enters*)
　Run, run,
　Bring the wool.
　I feel them coming
　Covered with mud.
　Bodies stiff,
　And the white sheet
　Heavy as marble.

　She goes. Enter Leonardo's Wife and Mother-in-law.

First Girl Are they coming?

Mother-in-law We don't know.

Second Girl What happened at the wedding?

First Girl Tell us.

Mother-in-law Nothing.

Wife I want to go back. I want to know everything.

Mother-in-law
  Go to your house. Stay there,
  Brave and alone.
  Grow old and weep.
  Keep the door shut.
  Shut out everybody,
  Dead and living.
  We'll seal the windows.
  Let the rains and the nights
  Fall on the bitter weeds.

Wife What has happened?

Mother-in-law
  It doesn't matter.
  Veil your face.
  Your children are your children.
  Nothing else. On your bed
  Put a cross of ashes
  Where his pillow was.

  They leave.

Beggar Woman (*at door*) Little girls. Is there a bit of bread?

Little Girl Go away.

Beggar Woman Why?

Little Girl We don't like your voice. Go away.

First Girl Don't be so rude.

Beggar Woman
I could have asked for your eyes.
A cloud of birds follows me.
Do you want one?

Little Girl I want to go home.

Second Girl (*to Beggar Woman*) Take no notice of her.

First Girl Did you come by the stream?

Beggar Woman I did.

First Girl O. Can you tell us –

Beggar Woman I saw them. They'll soon be here. Two
torrents lying without a movement, among the great
stones. Two men at the feet of a horse. Dead in the beauty
of the night. Dead, yes, dead.

First Girl Oh, I can't bear to hear it.

Beggar Woman
Their eyes broken flowers.
Their teeth two fistfuls
Of frozen snow.
They fell together
And the bride returns
With their blood in her hair,
And on her skirt.
They're coming now,
Covered by blankets,
Carried by tall young men.
It happened. And that's it.
And it was right.
Over the golden flower, dirty sand.

She goes. Girls begin to go.

First Girl
Dirty sand.

Second Girl
On the golden flower.

Little Girl
On the golden flower.
They're bringing the dead from the river,
One dark-skinned,
The other, dark-skinned.
Over the the golden flower
The shadow of a nightingale
Flutters and sobs.

*All go. Mother and Neighbour enter. Neighbour
sobbing.*

Mother Be quiet.

Neighbour I can't help it.

Mother I said be quiet. (*At the door*) Is anybody there?
(*Puts her hands to her forehead.*) My son should have
answered. But my son's nothing now – an armful of dry
flowers. A faint voice the other side of the mountains.
(*Angrily to Neighbour*) Will you be quiet. I want no
weeping in this house. Your tears are just tears, they come
from your eyes. My tears will be different. When I'm alone
my tears will come from the soles of my feet. From my
very roots. And they'll burn hotter than blood.

Neighbour Come with me to my house. You can't stay here.

Mother I want to be here. Here. Peaceful. Now they're all
dead. At midnight I'll sleep. And I shan't be afraid of a gun
or a knife. Other mothers will go to their windows, lashed
by the rain, looking for the faces of their sons. Not me.

And out of my sleep I'll make a cold marble dove to carry
camellias of frost to the graveyard. No, not to the
graveyard. It's not a graveyard. It's a bed of earth, a cradle
that shelters them and rocks them in the sky.

Enter woman in black, who kneels.

Mother (*speaking to Neighbour*) Take your hands from
your face. Terrible days are ahead. I don't want to see
anybody. The earth and me. My grief and me. And these
four walls. Oh! (*She sits.*)

Neighbour Have pity on yourself.

Mother I must be calm. The neighbours will be in here
and I don't want them to see me so poor. Everything gone.
A woman without one son to press to her lips.

Bride enters, without orange blossom, in black shawl.

Neighbour Where are you going?

Bride Here.

Mother Who is it?

Neighbour You see who it is.

Mother Do I? But I don't want to recognise her, or I shall
sink my teeth in her throat. Viper! (*She moves menacingly
towards the Bride, stops. To Neighbour*) Look at her
there, weeping, and me calm and not tearing her eyes out.
I can't understand it. Does it mean I didn't love my son?
But what about his honour? What's happened to his
honour? (*She strikes Bride, who falls.*)

Neighbour For God's sake! (*Tries to hold Mother.*)

Bride Leave her. I came here so she could kill me. So they
can carry me off with them. But not with your hands. Kill
me with iron hooks, with a sickle, and with such force you
break it on my bones. Let her go. I want her to know that

68

I'm clean. And though I'm mad they can bury me and no man will have looked at himself in the whiteness of my breasts.

Mother I don't want to hear it. What does that matter to me?

Bride Because I went off with the other one. Yes, I went. You would have done the same. I was a woman on fire. Inside and outside ablaze with agonies. Your son was a single drop of water that I hoped would give me children, and health: the other was a dark big river, carrying torn-up trees, that brought me the sound of its reeds and its song. And I was going with your son, your little boy of cold water. But the other sent thousands of birds that stopped me and dropped frost into the wounds of this poor, shrivelling woman, this girl possessed by flames. I didn't want to! Do you hear me? I didn't want to. My whole hope was your son and I haven't deceived him. But the other's arm dragged me like a wave from the sea. And it would always have dragged me, always, even if I'd been an old woman and all your son's sons had tried to hold me down by my hair.

Enter a neighbour.

Mother She's not to blame. And it's not my fault either. So who's to blame? A frail, delicate woman who sleeps badly and throws away a crown of orange blossom to find a patch of mattress warmed by another woman.

Bride Stop talking. Take your revenge. Here I am. Here's my throat. You see how soft it is. Easier than cutting a dahlia in your garden. But no. I am pure. Pure as a new-born child. And strong enough to prove it. Light the fire. We'll put our hands into the flames. You for your son. Me, for my body. I shall last longer.

Enter another neighbour.

Mother What does your honour matter to me? What do I care about your death? What do I care about anything? Blessed be the wheat, because my sons lie under it. Blessed be the rain, because it wets the faces of the dead. Blessed be God, because he lays us all together, so we can rest.

Another neighbour enters.

Bride Let me weep with you.

Mother Weep if you like. But there by the door.

Little Girl enters. Bride at door.

Wife (*entering*)
He was a handsome horseman.
Now he's a mound of snow.
He rode to fairs and mountains
And women's arms.
Now his brow is crowned
With the moss of night.

Mother
Your mother's sunflower,
Mirror of the earth.
Let them put a cross
Of bitter oleander
Upon your breast.
Over you a sheet
Of shining silk.
And let the water
Shape its weeping
Between your fingers.

Wife
Four young men
With weary shoulders

Bride
Four splendid youths

70

Carry death
Slowly through the air.

Mother
Neighbours.

Little Girl
Here they come.

Mother
It's the same.
The Cross, the Cross.

Women
Sweet nails,
Sweet Cross
Sweet name
Of Christ.

Bride
Let the Cross protect the dead and the living.

Mother
Neighbours. With a knife,
With a small knife,
On an appointed day
Between two and three in the morning,
Two men who were in love
Killed each other.
With a knife,
With a small knife
That hardly fits the hand
But slides in cleanly
Through surprised flesh
Till it stops
There,
In the quivering
Dark
Roots

Of the scream.

Here is a knife,
A small knife
That barely fits the hand,
Fish without scales or river,
On an appointed day
Between two and three in the morning
This knife
Left two men stiffening
With yellow lips.
It barely fits the hand
But slides in cold
Through startled flesh
Till it stops, there,
In the quivering
Dark
Roots
Of the scream.